It stretches as it always has stretched, in one thick enormous curving river of grass, to the very end. This is the Everglades.
—Marjory Stoneman Douglas

*"Unless this area is quickly established as a national park,
the wildlife there will become extinct."*
—George Melendez Wright,
Wildlife Division, U.S. National Park Service

To my mother, who instilled in me
a love of Florida's tropical light.
And to the students of Marjory Stoneman
Douglas High School, for finding ways to
heal in that light. —S. N. W.

For my parents,
Margaret and Brian,
who believed in me when others didn't.
—R. G.

All quotations in green or blue are those of Marjory Stoneman Douglas. Source notes can be found in the back of the book.

SIMON & SCHUSTER BOOKS FOR YOUNG READERS
An imprint of Simon & Schuster Children's Publishing Division • 1230 Avenue of the Americas, New York, New York 10020
Text copyright © 2020 by Sandra Neil Wallace • Illustrations copyright © 2020 by Rebecca Gibbon
• For information about special discounts for bulk purchases, please contact Simon & Schuster Special Sales
at 1-866-506-1949 or business@simonandschuster.com. • The Simon & Schuster Speakers Bureau can bring authors to your live event. For more
information or to book an event, contact the Simon & Schuster Speakers Bureau at 1-866-248-3049 or visit our website at www.simonspeakers.com.
Book design by Lizzy Bromley • The text for this book was set in Catalina Clemente. • The illustrations for this book were rendered in acrylic inks and
colored pencils. • Manufactured in China • 0921 SCP • 2 4 6 8 10 9 7 5 3
Library of Congress Cataloging-in-Publication Data • Names: Wallace, Sandra Neil, author. | Gibbon, Rebecca, illustrator.
Title: Marjory saves the Everglades : the story of Marjory Stoneman Douglas / Sandra Neil Wallace ; illustrated by Rebecca Gibbon.
Description: First edition. | New York : Simon & Schuster Books for Young Readers, an imprint of Simon & Schuster Children's Publishing Division,
2020. | "A Paula Wiseman Book." | Includes bibliographical references and index. | Audience: Ages 4–8. | Audience: Grades 2–3. | Summary: "The true story
of Marjory Stoneman Douglas, who saved the Florida Everglades from development and ruin"—Provided by publisher.
Identifiers: LCCN 2019053677 (print) | LCCN 2019053678 (ebook) | ISBN 9781534431546 (hardback) | ISBN 9781534431553 (ebook)
Subjects: LCSH: Douglas, Marjory Stoneman—Juvenile literature. | Conservationists—Florida—Biography—Juvenile literature. | Authors, American—20th
century—Biography—Juvenile literature. | Nature conservation—Florida—Everglades—Juvenile literature. | Wetland conservation—Florida—History—
Juvenile literature. | Environmental policy—United States—History—20th century—Juvenile literature. | Everglades (Fla.)—Juvenile literature.
Classification: LCC QH31.D645 W35 2020 (print) | LCC QH31.D645 (ebook) | DDC 333.72092 [B]—dc23
LC record available at https://lccn.loc.gov/2019053677 • LC ebook record available at https://lccn.loc.gov/2019053678

MARJORY
Saves the Everglades

Written by Sandra Neil Wallace   Illustrated by Rebecca Gibbon

A Paula Wiseman Book • Simon & Schuster Books for Young Readers
New York London Toronto Sydney New Delhi

Before airplanes and automobiles,
a girl in gold-rimmed glasses sailed
on a steamboat to Florida.

In a grove ripe with dimpled fruit, she bit into an orange—sweet and sticky.

Far from home and safe in her father's arms, young Marjory Stoneman shared his hazel eyes and a thirst for the tropical light. Now a seed was planted for her love of Florida.

But it would be a long time before Marjory felt the southern sunlight again. Or her father's warm hug.

After the trip, she trekked to Taunton with her mother. Back to apple trees and snow. They lived with her grandparents and Aunt Fanny, in a house with an attic window facing the stars.

While the grown-ups talked, talked, talked, Marjory climbed quietly into the attic and read, read, read. Books became her best friends.

*"I read a lot of things
I didn't understand,
but that didn't stop me."*

So did the outdoors.
In the winter, she hopped on her red bicycle and rode into the forest to find a Christmas tree.

In springtime, she watched herring flip-flopping in the Taunton River. Slow and steady at first, then WHOOSH like a tidal wave, flapping against the current, to lay their eggs.

When Marjory turned eighteen, she zoomed to Wellesley College. She wrote to Mother and Aunt Fanny about the mighty oak trees turning scarlet. But she never forgot the seed that had been planted when she was a child.

As more seasons passed, twenty-four-year-old Marjory married, but the union failed. She kept the Douglas name and boarded a train, leaving her old life behind.

Heading south, the train twisted and turned through forests of pine.

While Marjory slept, it *chug-chugged* toward palm trees. By morning, a tropical light, familiar and bright, woke her up.

Marjory's heart beat faster as the train screeched to a stop. She'd arrived at her destination: Miami, Florida.

A kind man with graying hair hopped aboard and strode toward her. "Hello, Father," she said. And just like that, after nineteen years of never seeing him, Marjory hugged her father.

"There we were reunited with no fuss and feathers."

Marjory's father had started the *Miami Herald* newspaper. He asked her to be a reporter. She couldn't wait to begin.

"Two or three reporters is all we had.
I was the only woman."

Finally she found her voice. It wasn't her father's voice, her mother's voice, or Aunt Fanny's. It was entirely the voice of Marjory Stoneman Douglas.

She wrote about schools of mullet leaping over Biscayne Bay. Sandy streets, shimmering like "moonlight on snow." And how women should have the right to vote, the same as men.

In 1917, with World War I raging in Europe, Marjory longed to write about the women joining the war effort. But no woman from Florida had enlisted in the navy, so Marjory did!

*"I wanted my own life
in my own way."*

Soon she joined the Red Cross and sailed for Europe. She wrote about refugees living in caves. They'd lost their homes because of the war. Marjory gave them what comfort she could: warm pajamas and powdered milk.

When the war ended, she returned to Florida but hardly recognized it. Workers dynamited, dug, and drained waterways to build, build, build.

"Trains, boats, automobiles arrived jammed with people."

Developers saw the soggy muck of the Everglades as useless swampland. "Drain the Everglades," they insisted. Speculators snapped up land by the gallon.

Marjory didn't want the old Florida she knew to disappear, so she decided to write about it. She studied its rare birds.
She searched for secluded beaches, swimming under the moonlight.

She *putt-putted* along Florida's new highway with her friends—right to the edge of the Everglades. They fished for breakfast and cooked it on a fire. Munching on garfish, Marjory watched the sun rise, giant and orange, then flamingo pink.

"The grass and the islands of the hardwoods stood alone in the light and the beautiful air."

But, at forty years old, Marjory had never been *inside* the Everglades, until she met gardener Ernest Coe.

Coe believed that the Everglades had to be preserved before they disappeared forever. He read how much Marjory knew about the birds and the fish.

Would she go on a trip to help him convince park officials to make the Everglades a national park?

Marjory couldn't wait to go! But having never lived outdoors, she packed for a party instead of a camping trip.

Traveling by houseboat, Marjory meandered through the Glades in a string of pearls, and a silk dress with pleats as thick as the saw grass jutting through the shallow waters.

She spotted crocodiles swimming, alligators soaking up the sun, and the wiry roots of ghost orchids wrapped around the trunks of pond apples.

She saw sea turtles round as rain barrels bobbing through forests of gumbo-limbo.

Soon Marjory was covered in mosquito bites.
She didn't care.
She'd fallen in love with the Everglades.

The people from the National Park Service felt differently. "A swamp is a swamp," they complained, swatting at mosquitoes. Where were the mountains, the canyons, and the rushing waterfalls? Who would ever visit the bug-infested Everglades?

At night, as manatees slept near the houseboat, hunters sailed silently by, hoisting fiery torches. They headed for the rookeries to snatch egrets and sell their feathers for women's hats.

Marjory knew that the Everglades had to become a national park to save the birds, the plants, and the other wildlife.

But without majestic mountains and bug-free canyons, how would she persuade park officials to love Florida's birds the way she did, and to protect them?

What if they could somehow *fly* with the birds? That was the answer—riding in the sky in a giant balloon!

UP, UP, the dirigible rose, with Marjory and the group in it, floating above the Everglades.

Below them, the shallow waters gleamed amber, curling through green-and-yellow prairies and sandhills of ziziphus. Coiling around tree islands of red and black mangroves. Arching across South Florida, like the tentacles of a giant squid.

It was all so beautiful and unique. For once, Marjory had no words to describe it.

Marjory and the others floated, free as birds, while the throaty sounds of fire plumes *puff-puffed* to keep them aloft.

In the late afternoon, the sounds of birds flying home drowned out the *thrum-thrumming* of the engine's flames.

Sky became feathers. Wood storks circled. Egrets and ibis swooped and dived. Marjory recognized all of them.

Ten, twenty, thirty thousand birds cast shadows against the pink sky.

The park officials had never seen so many birds in one place. By the time the sun had set, they'd forgotten about canyons and mountains. Marjory, Ernest Coe, and the birds had convinced them to make the Everglades a national park.

The ride in the sky stayed with Marjory long after her mosquito bites had healed. She built a curious cottage perfect for one person, plus several cats. She painted the walls flamingo pink.

Under its roof, which coiled and curled like the Everglades waters, Marjory studied her house cats and thought of the Florida panther.

Were the Everglades really a swamp? Marjory didn't think so. How could a place where flamingos flocked and thatch palms thrived be swampland, where water stood still? Marjory had to find out.

But in the 1940s, there wasn't much scientific research
on how the Everglades worked.
    Marjory asked geologists and anthropologists mountains
of questions.

She examined the Everglades muck, wearing a hat made of straw, never feathers. She learned about limestone sandcastles tunneling below the mud.

Fifty-seven-year-old Marjory dug deep, deep, deep into her research and made a monumental discovery.

The Everglades weren't a swamp at all, but a river. A slow-moving, life-giving *river of grass.*

"With those three words I changed everybody's knowledge."

Fresh water into salt water. Pinelands into lowlands. From the Kissimmee River into Lake Okeechobee, the Everglades teemed with life.

It supported so many kinds of life that it formed its own ecosystem, an ecosystem kept alive by water that Floridians depended on.

"*There are no other Everglades in the world.*"

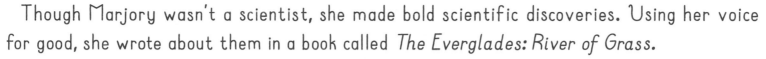

Though Marjory wasn't a scientist, she made bold scientific discoveries. Using her voice for good, she wrote about them in a book called *The Everglades: River of Grass*.

With language so lovely and logical, Marjory changed people's minds about the Everglades. For the first time, they knew why the Everglades mattered.

"Wherever fresh water runs and the saw grass starts up, that's where you have the Everglades."

LANDS NOW BEING RECLAIMED
RICHEST SOIL IN THE
WORLD.
DEEP MUCK, BIG CROPS, YEAR
ROUND. BUY NOW AT GROUND
FLOOR PRICES.
REALITY SECURITIES CORPORATION

But the mighty builders from the US Army had different plans for the Everglades. They straightened the natural curves of the Kissimmee River to control its water. The ancient river became a canal. They called it C-38.

Lake Okeechobee became polluted. Birds died. The Everglades began to dry up.
Marjory was heartbroken.

"The Everglades were dying."

And now there were plans to build a gigantic airport ... a jetport. RIGHT IN THE MIDDLE OF THE EVERGLADES! Cementing curves where water flowed and crocodiles and alligators swam.

Marjory's friend Joe Browder was trying to stop the jetport. He knocked on the door of her curious cottage and asked for help.

But "I'm just one person," she replied. "No one would pay any attention to me."

Joe drove Marjory to the jetport site. One runway had already been built.

By now, Marjory's eyesight had grown weak. The stronger, bigger glasses she wore didn't help much.

As she walked toward the runway, shafts of brilliant, tropical light caught the corners of Marjory's eyes where she could still see. She walked in this glow until a giant fence with a great big sign stopped her.

THE WORLD'S FIRST ALL-NEW JETPORT FOR THE SUPERSONIC AGE, it read.

Marjory knew that "supersonic" meant the end of the Everglades. She had to find a way to stop it.

"People only listen to organizations," she whispered to Joe.

"Why don't you start an organization?" he asked.

Marjory was almost eighty years old. She was nearly deaf and blind. But making a difference had nothing to do with those things.

At that moment, as ibis flew above her, their wings flapping like the sound of a thousand silken ribbons, and raindrops *tatta-tat-tapped* on her straw hat, Marjory became an activist.

"Every time it rains, we know the Everglades are there."

She started Friends of the Everglades.

Marjory and her Everglades friends rode around Lake Okeechobee in an old camper.

Motoring from town to town, Marjory told the residents why the jetport must be stopped and how important the Everglades were to Florida. "No matter how poor my eyes are I can still talk," Marjory said.

Three hundred people became Friends of the Everglades, then six thousand! Children and grown-ups. Anyone could join for a dollar.

"Be a nuisance," Marjory urged her Everglades friends. "Never give up."

The jetport builders didn't take Marjory seriously. They joked that they'd give earmuffs to the alligators, so the jumbo jets wouldn't disturb them. "We're going to build the jetport," they warned Marjory, "whether you like it or not."

But the governor of Florida and the president of the United States took Marjory very seriously. They pored over a study that found what Marjory already knew: The jetport would destroy the Everglades. Marjory and the study convinced the president that the jetport was a bad idea, and the jetport was stopped!

As the years passed, people forgot about the jetport. Sugar cane farmers reclaimed the Everglades water for their crops. Land developers drained more Everglades muck to build new towns. Most of all, they wanted Marjory to stop talking about saving the Everglades and its water.

"People must come to realize that it's all the same water, from the Kissimmee to Okeechobee to the Everglades."

Ninety-three-year-old Marjory refused to be silent. As mosquitoes buzzed and bit at town meetings, she spoke her mind.

"Go home, granny!" people yelled and hissed. "Butterfly chaser!" They booed.

"Can't you boo any louder than that?" Marjory demanded. "I've got all night, and I'm used to the heat."

Whenever Marjory spoke, she spoke the truth, no matter how unpopular her words were.

"If the Everglades go, then South Florida becomes a desert," Marjory explained.

What Marjory wanted for the Everglades was radical, enormous, and monumental. It was something that only Marjory dared to dream. What the Everglades needed, Marjory knew, was to be made whole again.

"The Everglades is a test. If we pass it, we get to keep the planet."

After nearly one hundred years of dredging, draining, and polluting, Marjory convinced the government to restore the Everglades. They worked to put the Everglades back to the way they'd found it. It became the largest restoration project in American history.

Engineers tore up the canals they had built. They filled in the ditches and gave the Everglades back its curves.

Soon, water meandered through South Florida.

Saw grass became submerged.

The birds came back. Ibis and egrets and wood storks.

So did the sea turtles, the crocs, and the alligators.

Returning the Everglades to what it was always meant to be—

a river of grass.

One person *had* made a difference. Slow and steady at first, then WHOOSH like a tidal wave, Marjory Stoneman Douglas saved the Everglades.

Author's Note

MARJORY STONEMAN DOUGLAS didn't intend to write about the Everglades, let alone save it. But when she returned to Florida after World War I, she hardly recognized it. The Florida that Marjory knew was rapidly disappearing—the rare orchids, magnificent birds, and massive trees along with it.

Marjory *had* to do something. When she became a journalist in 1915, she'd discovered a self-confidence she never knew she possessed. Facing the Florida legislature, she demanded that women must have the right to vote, but the male politicians didn't take her seriously. Fortunately, Florida conservationists did. Thanks to Marjory, a part of the Everglades became a national park, and the first park created not for sightseeing but for the benefit of animals and plants.

Back in the 1940s, few people knew what the word "ecology" meant. Marjory explained how destroying one part of the Everglades damaged the rest of Florida. She became the first person to make the world realize why the Everglades mattered.

After she wrote the book *The Everglades: River of Grass*, Marjory figured that the Everglades would be safe. It wasn't. That's when Marjory became an activist. She started Friends of the Everglades, and gave hundreds of talks on water, weather, and wetlands that make the Everglades healthy. She soon became hard of hearing and visually impaired because of age-related macular degeneration, and more vocal than ever in defending the Everglades, demonstrating the power of what one person can do right up to the age of 108. For years, Marjory, Friends of the Everglades, and members of the Seminole Tribe of Florida and the Miccosukee Tribe of Indians of Florida worked together to fight against legislation seeking to take Everglades land or pollute it. Several times they won and they keep winning today.

A wilderness area in Everglades National Park is named after Marjory Stoneman Douglas. So are environmental laws, buildings, and Marjory Stoneman Douglas High School in Parkland, Florida. The survivors of the fatal shooting there in 2018 didn't intend to become activists. But just as Marjory changed how people see the Everglades, students at her namesake school have changed the conversation about gun laws. They also learn and draw inspiration from Marjory by visiting Marjory's Garden, a botanical sanctuary they helped build on campus for hope and healing.

I found out about Marjory many years ago. As a journalist, I admired how she used her mind and her words to change the world. I wanted to write about Marjory Stoneman Douglas because she inspires me to use my own voice for good and to not make assumptions. The ability to be courageous, to be strong, and to lead an impactful life is in all of us at every moment that we are alive.

Today, half of Florida's original wetlands no longer exist. Everglades National Park is now a Biosphere Reserve for the United Nations Educational, Scientific, and Cultural Organization (UNESCO) and is also a UNESCO World Heritage Site. The park preserves 1.5 million acres of wetlands and eight distinct habitats, but the park is only 20 percent of the Everglades' original size. Because of human development, climate change, and hurricanes, the area is still fragile, and the fight to keep the Everglades healthy continues. Plants and animals tell the story of the Everglades' vitality. During her eighty-three years living in Florida and fighting for the Everglades, Marjory never forgot a plant or animal once she saw it. The protected, threatened, or endangered species found on these pages still exist in the Greater Everglades Ecosystem, thanks to Marjory and Everglades National Park. —S. N. W.

AMERICAN CROCODILE
The only place crocodiles and alligators coexist is in the Everglades.

GHOST ORCHID
Ghost orchids can take sixteen years to bloom, and they smell like soap.

WEST INDIAN MANATEE
Manatees eat tons of plants, keeping waterways clear.

FLORIDA SCRUB ZIZIPHUS
The lemon-like fruit of the ziziphus attracts butterflies and birds.

WOOD STORK
When water gets too low, wood storks stop nesting.

FLORIDA PANTHER
Florida's most endangered wild cat needs large areas to hunt.

GRFEN THATCH PALM
Its fan-shaped leaves give food and shelter to wildlife.

FLORIDA TREE SNAIL
This tiny mollusk feeds on fungus and is threatened by hurricanes and shell hunters.

FLORIDA LEAFWING BUTTERFLY
Their orange wings have brown undersides so they look like dead leaves and won't get eaten.

LEATHERBACK SEA TURTLE
The world's largest sea turtle sometimes gets tangled in fishing nets.

AMERICAN ALLIGATOR
Its thrashing tail digs holes in the sand, which later provide homes for other animals.

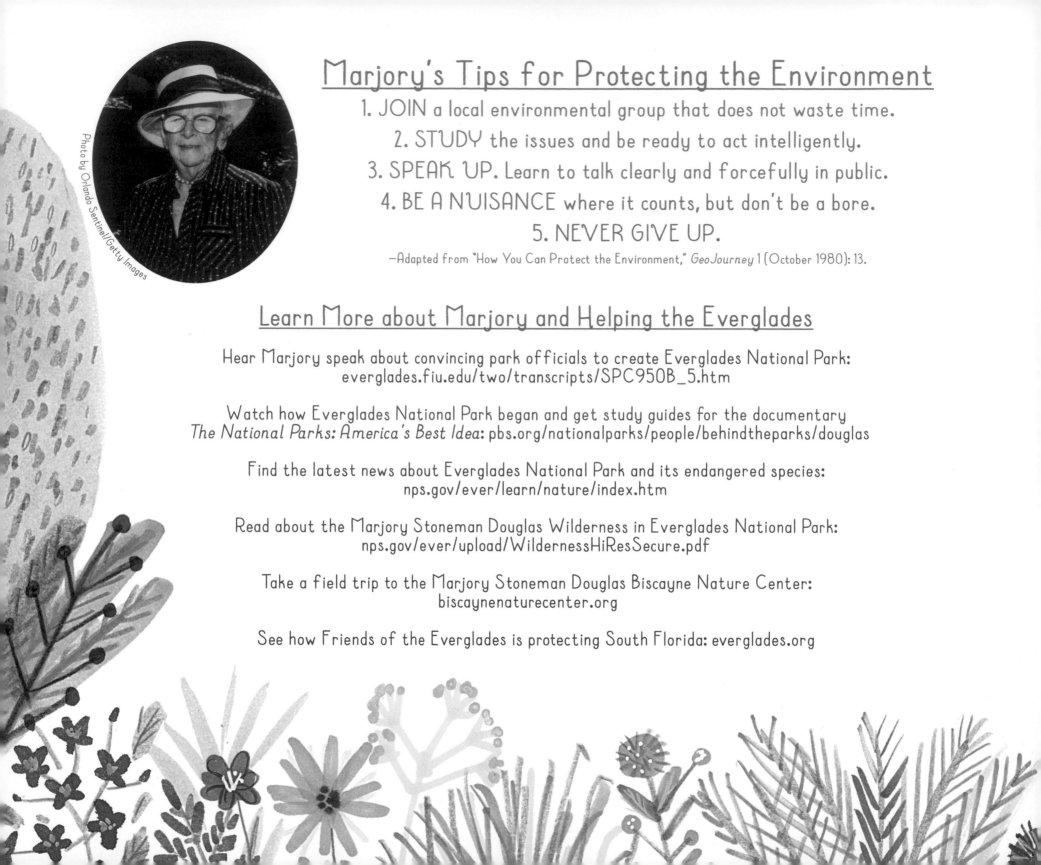

Marjory's Tips for Protecting the Environment

1. JOIN a local environmental group that does not waste time.

2. STUDY the issues and be ready to act intelligently.

3. SPEAK UP. Learn to talk clearly and forcefully in public.

4. BE A NUISANCE where it counts, but don't be a bore.

5. NEVER GIVE UP.

—Adapted from "How You Can Protect the Environment," *GeoJourney* 1 (October 1980): 13.

Learn More about Marjory and Helping the Everglades

Hear Marjory speak about convincing park officials to create Everglades National Park: everglades.fiu.edu/two/transcripts/SPC950B_5.htm

Watch how Everglades National Park began and get study guides for the documentary *The National Parks: America's Best Idea*: pbs.org/nationalparks/people/behindtheparks/douglas

Find the latest news about Everglades National Park and its endangered species: nps.gov/ever/learn/nature/index.htm

Read about the Marjory Stoneman Douglas Wilderness in Everglades National Park: nps.gov/ever/upload/WildernessHiResSecure.pdf

Take a field trip to the Marjory Stoneman Douglas Biscayne Nature Center: biscaynenaturecenter.org

See how Friends of the Everglades is protecting South Florida: everglades.org

Photo by Orlando Sentinel/Getty Images

Timeline of Marjory Stoneman Douglas and the Everglades

APRIL 7, 1890: Marjory Stoneman is born in Minneapolis, Minnesota.

1894: Marjory's mom and dad, Lillian and Frank Stoneman, take her on a trip to Havana, Cuba. They stop in Tampa, Florida, where Marjory picks oranges.

1896: Marjory's parents separate, and she moves with her mom to Taunton, Massachusetts. They live with Marjory's grandparents and Aunt Fanny.

1912: Marjory graduates from Wellesley, an all-women college where she majored in English composition. A few weeks after Marjory graduates, her mother dies of breast cancer.

APRIL 18, 1914: Marjory weds Kenneth Douglas, but the marriage is short-lived.

AUGUST 1914: World War I breaks out in Europe.

SEPTEMBER 1915: Marjory moves to Miami, Florida, and is reunited with her father. She becomes a newspaper reporter with the *Miami Herald*.

MARCH 27, 1917: Marjory makes history, becoming the first Florida woman to join the US Naval Reserve.

APRIL 1917: Marjory tries to convince members of the Florida state legislature to grant Florida women the right to vote, but is unsuccessful.

OCTOBER 1918: Marjory joins the American Red Cross and sails for Europe. She helps refugees displaced by World War I.

NOVEMBER 11, 1918: World War I ends.

1920: Marjory returns to Florida, where construction and Everglades dredging are changing water flow. She soon builds a cottage to blend in with nature and writes about the Everglades' rapidly declining habitat.

SEPTEMBER 18, 1926, AND SEPTEMBER 16, 1928: The Great Miami and Okeechobee Hurricanes strike South Florida, killing thousands of people and damaging the Everglades.

1930: Marjory joins conservationist Ernest Coe's committee to make the Everglades a national park. Riding in a Goodyear blimp, Marjory and Ernest Coe convince park officials to preserve the Everglades.

SEPTEMBER 1935: The Labor Day Hurricane, the most intense hurricane to hit landfall in US history, destroys much of the Florida Keys, killing more than four hundred people.

SEPTEMBER 1, 1939–SEPTEMBER 2, 1945: World War II

DECEMBER 6, 1947: President Harry S. Truman opens Everglades National Park. Three weeks earlier, *The Everglades: River of Grass*, written by Marjory, is published.

1962: The US Army Corps of Engineers straightens the Kissimmee River to control its water flow. Making the river into a canal called C-38 proves disastrous for South Florida.

1969: Marjory forms Friends of the Everglades, beginning her life as an environmental activist.

1990: Marjory Stoneman Douglas High School opens in Parkland, Florida.

1991: The Biscayne Nature Center is named after Marjory Stoneman Douglas.

AUGUST 1992: Hurricane Andrew, the most destructive hurricane to hit the US up to this date, destroys homes, kills forty-four people in Florida, and ruins thousands of acres in the Everglades.

1993: President Bill Clinton awards Marjory the Medal of Freedom, the nation's highest civilian honor.

1997: Much of Everglades National Park is named the Marjory Stoneman Douglas Wilderness.

The Comprehensive Everglades Restoration Plan (CERP) is created and eventually passed by Congress. Soon, the US Army Corps of Engineers works to restore the Everglades to its original curves and water flow, undoing some of the damage that the Corps caused by a hundred years of draining the Glades.

MAY 14, 1998: Marjory dies at the age of 108 in her Coconut Grove cottage.

Sources

"It stretches as it always has . . . This is the Everglades": Marjory Stoneman Douglas, *The Everglades: River of Grass* (Sarasota, FL: Pineapple Press, 2017), 10.

"Unless this area . . . wild life there will become extinct": George Melendez Wright, "Wright Indorses Park Plan to Protect 'Glades Wild Life," from the personal scrapbook of the George Melendez Wright family.

"I read a lot of things . . . that didn't stop me": Marjory Stoneman Douglas and John Rothchild, *Voice of the River* (Sarasota, FL: Pineapple Press, 1987), 52.

"Hello, father": Douglas and Rothchild, 96.

"There we were reunited with no fuss and feathers": Douglas and Rothchild, 96.

"moonlight on snow": Douglas and Rothchild, 99.

"Two or three reporters . . . I was the only woman": Douglas and Rothchild, 102.

"I wanted my own life in my own way": Douglas and Rothchild, 127.

"Trains, boats, automobiles arrived jammed with people": Douglas, *The Everglades*, 334.

"Drain the Everglades": Napoleon Bonaparte Broward quoted in Dayton Duncan and Ken Burns, *The National Parks: America's Best Idea: An Illustrated History* (New York: Alfred A. Knopf, 2009), 275.

"The grass and the islands . . . light and the beautiful air": Douglas and Rothchild, *Voice of the River*, 136.

"A swamp is a swamp": William T. Hornaday quoted in Duncan and Burns, *The National Parks*, 280.

"With those three words I changed everybody's knowledge": Douglas and Rothchild, *Voice of the River*, 191.

"There are no other Everglades in the world": Douglas, *The Everglades*, 5.

"Wherever fresh water runs . . . that's where you have the Everglades": Douglas and Rothchild, *Voice of the River*, 191.

"The Everglades were dying": Douglas, *The Everglades*, 349.

"I'm just one person . . . pay any attention to me": Tim Collie, "Marjory Stoneman Douglas, 'Voice of the River,'" *South Florida Sun Sentinel*, May 18, 1998.

"People only listen to organizations": Collie, "Marjory Stoneman Douglas."

"Why don't you start an organization?": Douglas and Rothchild, *Voice of the River*, 225.

"Every time it rains, we know the Everglades are there": Jack E. Davis, *An Everglades Providence: Marjory Stoneman Douglas and the American Environmental Century* (Athens, GA: University of Georgia Press, 2009), 476.

"No matter how poor my eyes are I can still talk": Douglas and Rothchild, *Voice of the River*, 230.

"Be a nuisance. . . . Never give up": Marjory Stoneman Douglas, "How You Can Protect the Environment," *Geo Journey* 1 (October 1980): 13.

"We're going to build . . . like it or not": Davis, *An Everglades Providence*, 487.

"People must come to realize . . . to Okeechobee to the Everglades": John Doussard, "It's Never Too Late for Anything," *Miami News*, February 6, 1981.

"Go home, granny!": Steven Yates, "Marjory Stoneman Douglas and the Glades Crusade," *Audubon*, March 1983, 113.

"Butterfly chaser!": Yates, "The Glades Crusade," 113.

"Can't you boo any louder than that?": Douglas and Rothchild, *Voice of the River*, 232.

"I've got all night, and I'm used to the heat": Yates, "The Glades Crusade," 113.

"If the Everglades go, then South Florida becomes a desert": Davis, *An Everglades Providence*, 522.

"The Everglades is a test. . . . get to keep the planet": Cheryl Devall, "Marjory Stoneman Douglas Remembered," *All Things Considered*, NPR, May 14, 1998, transcript.